MADE TO LEAD

A Pocket Guide to Managing Marketing & Creative Teams

Obligatory Disclaimer:
Applying this advice will likely help
you, but your mileage may vary (YMMV).

Ready to accelerate your progress?
Get free tools to accompany this book
at SakasAndCompany.com/teambook

Please send your questions, comments,
and feedback (even the typos!) to
Karl@SakasAndCompany.com

(*FAQ: It's pronounced "say-kiss."*)

ISBN: 1537639358
ISBN-13: 978-1537639352

Dedication

This book is dedicated to YOU, as a leader within a marketing agency, design studio, digital shop, or other creative firm.

Leading a team is tough. When you lead an entire company—a *team* of teams—it's even harder.

I believe leaders are *made*, not born. By reading this book, you're already taking the next step forward in your leadership and management journey. Your entire team will benefit from this choice. Nice job!

Karl Sakas

Agency Consultant
Raleigh, North Carolina, USA

Table of Contents

Foreword by Jay Baer

The agency business has never been easy, but it's now harder than ever. Technology-fueled disruption has spawned a modern maelstrom of change that leaves us bewildered, and breathless. But there's one element of the agency business that remains unchanged. In fact, it may be more true than it's ever been:

Your power is in your people.

I've worked in, managed, owned, and consulted with agencies for 28 years and I have concluded that there is no such thing as "secret sauce." The proprietary planning methodology you use to conjure smart strategies for clients? It's not proprietary. Nor is it particularly different from any other agency's version of the same.

The truth is that what agencies sell, how they sell it, and how they deliver and execute those assignments is manifestly the same. What makes ALL the difference—what makes your agency viable and vigorous and valid, and ultimately, victorious is the quality of your people and the quality of how you lead them.

Karl Sakas is a soothsayer. He can take one look at how the people of your agency collide and cooperate; how they integrate and intersect; and tell you whether you have effective leadership. He gets it. He's like the Dr. Phil of agency owners and managers: one part confidante, one part ass kicker.

Now, he's giving you the playbook directly. In *Made to Lead*, Karl shares dozens of wise and practical tips for how you can become a better agency leader, and how your people (and your firm) will blossom as a consequence. Some of these tips you may know. Some you may have forgotten. Others will be as yet unfamiliar. But I'm certain you'll benefit from them.

Jay Baer

President of Convince & Convert and author of *Hug Your Haters*

Bloomington, Indiana, U.S.A.

Acknowledgements

Thanks to my worst managers for showing me what *not* to do—and to my best managers for showing me the opposite.

Thanks to Cari Baldwin, Cathy Atkins, Courtney Hurst, Gabriella Rackoff, Leslie Camacho, Melissa Cohen, Mike Belasco, Patrick King, and Radhakrishnan Kg for your excellent advance-review feedback.

Thanks to Katie Connors, Melissa Breau, and Rachel Go for your ongoing advice and support. You make my work easier.

Thanks to Jason Moore, Jennifer Barnett, Lydia Stutzman, Sami Nummi, and Sara Parker at Fulcrum Creatives for your design and marketing help. You make things better.

Thanks to Paul Panfalone for your illustrations.

Thanks to Jay Baer for sharing the foreword.

Thanks to Alan Wishengrad, Evan Carroll, John Grinnell, Laura Westman, Mihali Stavlas, Stan Phelps and Ted Seward for helping me grow as a leader.

Thanks to Angela Williams, Earl Brooks, and Linda Slagle for inspiring my consulting.

Thanks to Barbara Blythe for being a great friend.

Thanks to my parents for my focus on results.

And thanks to *you* for buying and reading this book! I'm looking forward to hearing how you grow as a leader and a manager.

You're in the Right Place

Are you reading the right book? I hope so!

This book is for you if you work at an agency and oversee at least one person. Your title might be owner, partner, CEO, VP, director, project manager, account manager, or something else.

(Note: My language focuses on teams at agencies but most of the lessons still apply if you lead an in-house team.)

Let's get existential—you're also in the right place at work. You're managing because you own the agency or because the owners believe you're the right person for the job.

You may feel a sense of loss compared to your previous work as an individual contributor.

As a manager, you often go home without seeing tangible results of your work.

Your work has changed—I'll share how to make this easier.

Why I Wrote This Book

I wrote this book because managing people is tough—but it doesn't have to be so hard! It's easier when you have the right mindset and the right tools.

In my own experience as a manager, my natural inclination is to focus too much on the end result, on reaching the goal. That's good for productivity as an individual contributor…but not for team morale when you're the leader.

In 2012, I received a sobering set of 360° feedback from bosses, peers, and subordinates over the past decade. In summary, I was **good at getting things done, but not at making them fun.**

Or as another participant at the leadership retreat observed:

> "You can't be a leader if no one wants to follow you."

Shaken, I committed to do better—to add structure, to change my behavior, and to constantly find ways to improve.

It's a work in progress, but my leadership ratings have improved since then. I solicit feedback and am continuously improving. Each day is a new opportunity.

The advice in this book comes from my experience as an agency leader, manager, individual contributor, board president, and agency consultant.

I've worked in digital marketing for two decades—since 1997—and I've learned plenty of lessons the hard way. I've also seen the successes and mistakes of my clients—leaders at digital agencies on six continents.

If you can make better decisions as a leader and a manager, it's a win for you and for your team.

Why to Read This Book

It's especially hard when it feels like you were forced into doing a job—"boss" or "manager"— that you never wanted in the first place. I get it.

Yet if people report to you, you're a manager. You can deny reality but that's not very productive. Instead, recognize that you're in a unique position to improve the lives of your team.

If it feels like you don't know everything, that's OK. I've advised agency leaders around the world and discovered leaders are made, not born.

Leading and managing comes more easily to some than others, but I know from my experience as a manager that anyone can improve.

By reading this book, you're already ahead—you want to improve, and so you will improve. I'm excited to join you on your management and leadership journey!

Good management is about getting results through other people. You're still working hard yourself, but as a manager, your primary job is to inspire and lead your team to get things done. Your team can accomplish far more than you would by yourself— and far more than they'd accomplish without your guidance.

Whether you're new to management or a long-time manager, you'll find something for you in this book.

Indeed, many of these tips will not seem new or groundbreaking—but I mention them because I see so many leaders fail to follow them.

As 18th century author Samuel Johnson reminded us:

> "People need to be reminded more often than they need to be instructed."

Ready to accelerate your progress? Get free tools here: SakasAndCompany.com/teambook

Let me know how this book impacts you— email me at Karl@SakasAndCompany.com.

About Word Choices

A former boss joked that we were "separated by a common language"—that is, we *think* we're speaking the same language, but we make poor assumptions that lead to miscommunications.

Let's get on the same page about language. Specifically, let's look at whether you're an agency, and whether you're a leader or a manager.

Agency (or Studio or Shop or...)

You might call yourself a marketing agency, a creative studio, a development shop, a PR firm, a video production house, or something else.

My view? **You're an agency** if your company does creative or marketing work for hire (that is, for paying clients).

Ultimately, you're a services company delivering an intangible, creative-ish service whose quality depends highly on your team's expertise and delivery.

Leader vs. Manager

Most people see leaders as the person at the very top of an organization—in the board room and the corner office—while managers work in cubicles handling day-to-day operations.

In that model, leaders are in a glamorous strategic role, while managers are in the boiler room prodding their employees to submit their timesheets.

For our purposes here, **I consider "leader" and "manager" to be interchangeable.**

Good managers think like leaders—sharing their vision with the team to reduce or eliminate micromanagement.

Good leaders think like managers—choosing strategies that are workable in the real world.

Let's dive in!

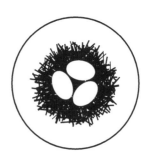

PART I:

Attitude &
Acceptance

My grandfather was a business professor and management consultant for 40+ years. His specialty was helping large corporations work more cooperatively with their employees.

In his research on managers in the 1950s, he observed that employees wished their manager would get to know them as people instead of just workers.

That's to say, we've known this for at least 60 years. But *knowing* is not *doing*. Can you name each employee's partner, kids, pets, etc.?

Your employees want you to get to know them, and they want to get to know you, too.

Are you approaching management with the right attitude? This section explores the topic.

As a manager, accept that your job is to get results through other people.

As a manager, you'll do plenty of roll-up-your-sleeves work yourself, but your team's success is your success.

If you're doing *everything* yourself, you're *not* doing your job as the manager. Instead, set a vision, hold your team accountable, and coach people along the way.

This is different from your work before, where you had physical or digital "artifacts" each day.

Venture capitalist Paul Graham refers to this as "maker" vs. "manager." Makers need uninterrupted time to create. Managers, in contrast, work in 30- and 60-minute timeslots.

As a manager, your team's output is your output. Miss having tangible results? Take up a physical hobby outside of work, unless you find gratification from how packed your calendar looks.

(2)

Begin with the end in mind.

————

Stephen Covey popularized the concept of "begin with the end in mind." If you know where you're going, you can work backwards to get there. Share your vision with the team, so you can inspire the team to support your vision.

To structure this, I created a visualization tool called an "Advance Retrospective." In short, you write about the future as if it's already happened.

Start by referencing a future date—a year away, five years away, a milestone birthday. For instance, open with: **"Today is December 31, 20XX. It's a great day because..."**

Most people describe the things they do, the people they work with, and how they feel. Advance Retrospectives tend to be one to three pages long, but you can write as much or as little as you want.

Try it! Once you know where you want to go, you can work backwards from there.

Make your team the Heroes, with you as the important (but secondary) Helper.

In mythology expert Joseph Campbell's "Hero's Journey" model, the Hero embarks on a difficult journey, defeats a major villain or other obstacle, and returns home as an improved person.

Along the way, they'll have a Helper—like Han Solo in *Star Wars*, or like Hermione and Ron in *Harry Potter*.

When you're in a high-responsibility role, it's easy to see *yourself* as the Hero—but that's not the right approach. On your team, your employees are the Heroes, and you're their Helper. For your team, *clients* should be the Heroes, with your employees as the Helpers.

As my dad advised me in middle school, "Leaders eat last." Take care of your team— "servant leadership" is more sustainable than "command-and-control."

4

Apply "Warmth & Competence" in your management style.

Competence is getting the job done. Warmth is showing you care about people, that you see them as individuals instead of cogs in a machine.

Going beyond you, this is an important value to demonstrate to your client-facing team.

Why? Because clients are more likely to fire your agency for a bad client experience (Low Warmth) than doing bad work (Low Competence). And a pattern of High Warmth means your client will give your team the benefit of the doubt the first time something goes wrong.

For more on Warmth & Competence, read *The HUMAN Brand* by former Fortune 500 CMO Chris Malone and Princeton psychology professor Susan T. Fiske.

5

Create—and spend—
a budget for team morale.

You can make a big impact on a relatively small budget.

If you have five direct reports, spending $1,000 a year would cover birthday cards, the first round of monthly drinks, and three $20 "spot award" gift cards per employee every year.

Also, be sure the gift cards are for a place *they* like, not a place *you* like.

Most good management is free—throwing in some cash occasionally can sweeten the deal. However, be careful about setting precedents; once you start, it hurts morale to stop.

Don't try to have all the answers. You won't. And that's OK.

There are some things people need to know—for instance, an account manager leading a client's monthly review meeting should know key results from the past month. But you don't need to memorize everything.

For random questions, show your team it's OK to say, "Let me check on that; I'll get back to you by tomorrow morning."

Make it safe. Research at Google found that "psychological safety"—a shared belief that team members can take interpersonal risks—is a key factor at successful teams.

PART II:

Coaching & Development

Have you ever had an employee quit? It's stressful. Even when you're glad they're leaving, you still need to deal with their workload. You want someone to start ASAP.

Early in my career as an agency leader, I got an email from a grad student. She was finishing her program and wanted to learn about jobs at my agency. I said "yes"—but warned I wasn't hiring.

Over coffee, she shared some great lessons learned from her agency internship that weren't on her résumé. She said she'd keep in touch, and did.

A few months later, one of my employees quit to take an in-house role.

We got over 100 applications for the entry-level role—but I ultimately hired the now-graduated student based on her initiative and experience. Years later, she now leads a department at a fast-growing agency in the Inc 5000.

Let's look at how you can find and develop great employees.

Hire "New Rope"
instead of "Wet Twine."

When you hire the *right* people, managing them is a lot easier. When you hire the *wrong* people, you make your job harder.

Use the "New Rope vs. Wet Twine" framework to make the decision easier, courtesy of customer experience expert Stan Phelps.

New Rope is reliable and strong. New Rope doesn't break. "New Rope" employees add value. They get the job done—faster and better than you expected. New Rope brings you solutions, not problems. In general, they put the company first.

In contrast, Wet Twine is unreliable and weak. Wet Twine is likely to break. "Wet Twine" employees make your life harder. They require close oversight and lots of reminders. Wet Twine tends to bring you problems instead of solutions. They often stir up drama, because they put themselves before the company.

When you hire reliable New Rope and don't hire flakey Wet Twine, managing is suddenly a lot easier.

Stop expecting your team to read your mind.

Your team can't read your mind.

Stop getting frustrated when employees aren't meeting your expectations…if you never set them.

Stop getting annoyed that employees keep asking you how to do something… if you've never explained the framework you use to make those decisions.

Stop complaining that rank-and-file employees keep asking questions about the agency's future… if you've only discussed those plans privately at executive meetings.

Instead, make sure people know your values, goals, and resources (VGR). They can use your VGR to make better decisions without needing to ask you every single time.

Get to know your team as individuals.

If you don't know the name of your employees' romantic partners and pets, it's probably a sign that people don't think you know them well. And if you have too many people to get to know them individually, you probably have too many direct reports—divide that up.

Most of this happens on a day-to-day basis—your taking a genuine interest in your employees' lives outside of work. But you can also accelerate the process with a survey.

When I led a two-day marketing conference, I built a 10-person leadership team. At the beginning of the year, I sent a survey around—getting everyone's birthday (so I could send cards), mailing address (so I could send notes), t-shirt size (for a t-shirt making exercise), snacks (for team meetings), adult beverages (likewise for meetings), hobbies and pets, and their goal(s) for the year.

Use "incentive alignment" in recruiting and management.

In life, people tend to do what they have the incentive to do—use that in your recruiting and management.

Perhaps someone wants to get promoted, or wants new responsibilities, or wants to prove themselves. Knowing these things, you can find a way to align their incentives with your incentives.

If you have something you need someone to do, and they want to do it because it advances their *own* goals—there's incentive alignment.

Be sure you aren't giving people the *wrong* incentives. Wells Fargo was fined $185 million in 2016 after the bank's employees had secretly opened two million accounts without customers' permission. It turns out employee compensation depended heavily on creating new accounts.

Regulator Richard Cordray said, "Unchecked incentives can lead to serious consumer harm, and that is what happened here."

Commit to helping your team improve.

In one of my anonymous Culture Surveys, agency employees shared they were frustrated at not getting specific feedback from their managers. They'd hear "that's good" or "that's bad" —when they *really* wanted guidance on *why* their deliverables were good or bad.

If someone does something well—or poorly—take the time to explain what worked and what didn't work. People can't improve if you don't explain the "why" behind it.

As a leader, you have an obligation to help your team members improve their leadership skills—so they can move to new roles in your agency and so they can improve as professionals.

Worried people will take your coaching and leave? Most eventually will—but you'll benefit from your efforts until then.

Creating internal "Office Hours" makes it easier to fit feedback into your schedule. More about that on page 41 plus public Office Hours on the next page.

Always Be Recruiting.

There's a saying that "people don't quit companies, they quit managers." Despite that, don't take it personally every time someone quits—you should learn from it, but don't dwell on it.

Instead, adopt an "Always Be Recruiting"mindset. When you're always on the lookout for future candidates, you won't be so concerned when someone quits—or when you need to fire a poor performer.

So, how can you meet people without filling your schedule with potentially low-value meetings? Start with your network—let people know you're always open to meeting top performers.

Next, create public "Office Hours" at a coffee shop near your office (that's what I do!). The idea is that anyone can drop in (or makean appointment) to chat—so that the meetings don't disrupt your schedule.

These also let you handle the "can I pick your brain?" requests—you can reply, "Sure, come to my weekly Office Hours. The next opening is X weeks from now."

Think about how your team members fit into the agency's leadership pipeline.

Do you know their goals? Helping employees reach their goals wins their loyalty.

Some people are happy to stay where they are. Others want to move up. Others want to move laterally.

If someone's goals include leaving (because they want to go back to school, because they don't want to stay agency-side, or something else), you should help them transition. It's the right thing to do— and pragmatically, it helps you move on to hire a replacement who's excited to be there.

This impacts employee retention. When I do anonymous Culture Surveys at agencies, employees often share that they believe the agency's future is bright… but they aren't sure how *they* fit into that future.

Think about your next move, because no one else will do that for you.

Your clients call you any time they want something. Your employees interrupt you with questions all day long. And vendors are always trying to sell you something.

But no one has ever called to remind you about what you need to do this week to prepare for three years in the future. (For my clients, I'm that person.)

It's important to occasionally block-off time occasionally (the beginning of the month, or at least the beginning of the quarter) to do check-ins on your goals and progress. No one else is going to remind you.

If you aren't strategic about this, you'll find yourself in a future you didn't choose. It's your life—I don't recommend depending on happy accidents.

PART III:

Meetings &
Communication

When you become a manager, your role in meetings changes. As an individual contributor, your job was mostly just to show up—to get updates and leave with to-dos.

As a manager, you're *running* the meeting—and that means you can't just show up. You shouldn't do most of the talking, but you ultimately set the agenda and the tone. This means you have the power to make meetings better—or worse—for everyone.

When you don't prepare for a meeting and waste an hour, you're wasting an hour times the number of people in the meeting. If you bill the equivalent of $150/hour and it's 10 people, you just burned $1,500.

A client shared that he was always leaving meetings with more to-dos. I gave him a challenge—to try to leave 80% of meetings with no personal to-dos.

So far, he's achieved this on client meetings (his team handles most follow ups), and he's made progress on internal meetings. The key is he's making an effort to change, versus letting meetings happen to him.

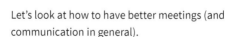

Let's look at how to have better meetings (and communication in general).

No one likes meetings. Apply meetings as needed, not to exceed X doses daily.

We've known for a long time that we have too many meetings. In my 1972 copy of *How to Run Better Business Meetings*, Chapter 2 is entitled "Is This Meeting Necessary?"

Meetings should be worthwhile—and frequency matters. Daily standups make sense for a project team. Weekly meetings make sense for a department. As your agency grows, move all-hands meetings from monthly to quarterly.

Ultimately, find the "X" frequency that works for you—meetings are like a version of Goldilocks and the Three Bears (not too little, not too much).

Meeting length matters, too. You don't want your team to feel like they're locked in a room for a time-share sales pitch.

Remember that meetings aren't just 30 or 60 or 90 minutes—they include prep time and followups. Think back to the 1972 book: "Is This Meeting Necessary?"

Have an agenda for your meetings, and be sure to balance work and fun.

You may have seen the meme online: "I survived another meeting that should have been an email."

Don't meet without an agenda—even if your agenda is just a handwritten list of topics you want to cover.

Before you have a meeting, think about what you want to accomplish. It's fine to share updates, but think about how to take it beyond a live email.

And make it fun! Fun for them, not you. Employees are there because they have to be there—don't take advantage of that. The right solution here will depend on your personality and your agency's culture.

If no one wrote it down, it's like it never happened.

Ensure someone's taking minutes at meetings. Meeting minutes don't have to be complicated, but they'll ideally include at least key lists— decisions and actionables.

Recording decisions protects you later if there's a disagreement. Actionables (including what, by when, by whom) help you make progress after the meeting.

If everyone leaves a meeting without decisions and/or actionables, why did you have the meeting?

Keep people updated...
but not too much.

———

Just because you *can* doesn't mean you *should*.

Ultimately, most people don't need to know every detail about what you're working on, but they *do* need to know what you're doing if it affects them.

On email, this means cc'ing the right people—and no more than that. If someone should be aware, you can use bcc or forward them a separate copy of the thread so they're not on the reply-all.

If you're using a group communications system, this means sharing things via the appropriate channel(s). Unless it truly needs to be private, lean toward sharing publicly within the tool—you never know when someone else should know something you're sharing (or could share an insight that improves your decision making).

Talk to your team before promising anything to a client.

———

Don't you hate it when someone promises you'll do something without asking you first? There's volunteering and there's "volun-told."

Don't be that person. If a client asks you something, it's totally fine to say "I'm not sure; let me ask the person who handles that"—you don't need to have an instant answer to every question.

Be sure your team knows this, and be sure you "model" the behavior yourself—check before you speak when you don't know the answer.

This is especially important about budget and scope questions, because poor answers cost you money. Train your team to say things like "Let me check with the PM on scope" and "Would you like an estimate for that?"

Close your "open door" policy.

As a leader, you shouldn't be getting constant interruptions. I mean, I'm not surprised if you *are*, but it has to stop.

Check email less often, disable background notifications, and train employees that if they're waiting on your feedback, it's up to *them* to follow up (and escalate if needed).

I know you know all of this. Yet when you don't act on it, it's the same as not knowing at all. Try cutting off communication for an hour or two at a time, and then keep extending. If something truly can't wait, train people to use your "emergency contact" method.

Don't be inaccessible—that's not good, either. One option is to have internal "Office Hours" a couple times a day where anyone can drop in with questions. The idea is your door is open at times.

You can learn a lot through "management by walking around." Informal chats can reveal challenges you might not hear formally.

Know when to choose synchronous vs. asynchronous communication.

It's easy to do everything via email, but emails aren't the right choice when you need to communicate something difficult or sensitive.

Ultimately, you're choosing whether you need *synchronous* communication (live, real-time) like a call or meeting—or *asynchronous* communication like email, posts in your PM software, or comments in a shared document.

Sometimes you need to choose the tougher channel—a live conversation—because it's the right method for the job. A live conversation means you and the other people can clarify in the moment.

If you always prefer email, remind yourself that conversations can produce a dramatically better result.

If you always prefer conversations for even routine updates, you should weigh whether it's worth interrupting your team.

Decide if you're the kind of manager who rewards "facetime"... or results.

When you expect everyone to be in the office five days a week, you're telling your team that you value "facetime" (seeing them at their desk) over results.

Smarter managers trust employees to be adults. This means giving people goals and parameters and letting them get things done.

If you're insisting someone be in the office, think whether that's really necessary. Sometimes it is. But not as often as most managers require.

If you're a "facetime" boss, embrace it—and accept that you're going to attract and retain lower-quality employees.

PART III:

Motivation & Accountability

Are your employees thinking like owners? They *should* be—because it helps make you "needed but not necessary."

I joined one of my teams for a reward dinner at the Angus Barn, a nice steakhouse in Raleigh, NC. As we finished our entrées, the dining room manager, Nancy, stopped by to see how we were doing.

One of my team members expressed irritation over the dessert options. A few minutes later, Nancy returned with a custom, off-menu dessert that perfectly met his needs. He went from annoyed to delighted.

I assumed Nancy was one of the owners. I checked afterwards—she wasn't an owner, but she *acted* like one. I found a company newsletter describing her approach—around creating a "pampering effect" for guests. The restaurant noted, "[Nancy] characterizes her role as that of the hostess of a huge dinner party who insists on perfection in every detail."

Find employees who think and act like owners—and empower them to take action. You'll love the results.

Hold yourself accountable—and track the team's progress, too.

When you make a promise to a team member, you need to follow through on it. If you don't, you're showing your team that integrity doesn't count.

Got lots of requests to juggle? Put the ball in their court—for instance, if they request something in a hallway conversation, ask them to follow up with you via email or your PM system. That is, the request hasn't officially happened 'til they've submitted it via your preferred channel.

This also includes accountability for your team—if someone says they'll accomplish something by a certain date and they haven't done it, it's not micromanagement for you to ask about the status.

When it's bonus time, everyone ideally can say, "I accomplished XYZ," not, "I showed up for a year."

Pad the schedule to allow extra lead time.

I've never regretted padding a schedule or timeline estimate.

Why? Because things always take longer than you expect. And when people *depend* on you, your bad estimates make their life harder.

Don't make your employees' lives harder—they will eventually quit. And don't deny reality—something's going to come up that makes things take longer than you initially expected.

When it's always an emergency, something's broken—and you're not being a good leader. By planning ahead, you can avoid needing to take "heroic measures."

If your team keeps asking what time it is, build them a clock. You want to make your self "needed but not necessary."

When people keep asking you the same questions, you need to find a way to answer the question once and for all.

This might come in the form of a Frequently Asked Questions (FAQ) resource or ensuring your team knows your Values, Goals, and Resources (VGR).

You won't eliminate *all* questions (and you don't *want* to). But when you "build a clock," you're pre-answering 80% of the questions your team might ask. When they know your VGR, they can make more decisions without requiring you every time.

This all contributes to making yourself "needed but not necessary." That's the ideal outcome as a manager—you can't disappear completely but you can step away and enjoy that two-week vacation.

Find a check-in process that focuses on results, not blame.

If someone's missed a deadline, ask them the new ETA. From that, ask what led to the missed deadline—from an attitude of support, not blame. It's not like you've never missed a deadline, right?

If you want to ask about something, I like the phrase "What's your sense of ETA on such-and-such?" (Of course, you're really thinking, "Where the *$*%& is the such-and-such?!?")

It worked? Credit your team.
It failed? Take the blame.

As a leader, one of your jobs is to protect your team against blowback when things go poorly. Nothing builds loyalty like standing up for a team member and saying, "That was my fault." Because it *was* your fault, because leaders are ultimately responsible for what happens on their watch.

On the praise side, this includes shoutouts to the rest of the team—as a leader, you look good when you say, "So-and-so created X."

You've worked hard to get where you are. Part of that means paying things forward.

Conduct debriefs (post-mortems) on projects, retainers, and internal initiatives.

Want to get better? You need to make time to do debriefs—and to learn from them. Knowing but not acting is like not knowing at all.

Debriefs work outside the agency world, too—for instance, surgical teams that do debriefs after each operation work faster while making fewer mistakes.

A debrief isn't complicated—you're answering three simple yet powerful questions:

#1 What worked?

#2 What didn't work?

#3 What should we do differently next time?

Consider involving clients—they'll be glad to share feedback—and be sure you learn from the debriefs.

Don't skip one-on-ones.

One-on-ones give your employees a chance to share concerns before those concerns grow. Yet I find that agency leaders often cancel their internal one-on-one meetings, saying they're too busy to meet.

This prioritization problem extends beyond meetings to include goals and performance evaluations. One client admitted it took him until July to give his managers their official annual goals for the currently-running year.

When you don't give your team guidance on goals or repeatedly cancel your one-on-one meetings, you're showing your employees they aren't important to you.

This hurts employee retention and keeps you from getting early insights into problems. Remember the power of "management by walking around."

Remember, saying "thank you" is free.

A paycheck only goes so far—take time to recognize people for what they've accomplished.

I do this through thank-you notes, recognition to the team via email and in person, and LinkedIn recommendations.

As president of AMA Triangle, I give a monthly award to the team member who best exemplifies our organization's values. Each recipient writes their own inspirational quote on the "Lantern Award" (literally an antique railroad lantern).

Little things make a big difference, as Stan Phelps describes in his "Purple Goldfish" book series.

I remember sending a specific thank-you note to an AMA Triangle volunteer. Afterwards, she shared that in working nearly 20 years in marketing, she had never received a thank-you note from a boss before.

Go order a box of thank-you notes right now.

Don't be afraid to fire people.

Firing shouldn't be your *first* solution, but it needs to be in your management toolbox.

For example, a client shared that his salesperson wasn't meeting her quota. He'd hired her 18 months earlier, to double his agency's revenues.

I asked how long she'd missed his quota. He replied, "18 months"—that is, she'd *never* met her quota. Not only did he waste her salary but he missed the Opportunity Cost of doubling his revenue.

What about your agency? Warn the employee first—and give them a chance to improve, ideally through a formal Performance Improvement Plan (PIP). But if problems continue, you need to part ways.

Firing someone is hard (notice a theme about management here?) but it's better than continuing to deal with the problems they cause.

By the time my clients fire someone, they usually wish they'd done it months earlier.

PART V:

Applying This at Your Agency

Good management is simple, but not easy.

Management is a process of continuous improvement—each of the tips here are basic enough. But have you ever met a manager who's mastered them *all*? I haven't!

In the real world, there are a lot of moving parts. It's tempting to just *avoid* managing—like your worst managers at past jobs, who didn't approach management as something they should at least attempt to master.

If you have a team, you're a manager—so I encourage you to commit to becoming better at it. Your commitment will help you eliminate drama, meet your long-term goals, and make life better for your employees and their families.

Let's make it happen!

Do three things today.

Want to see consistent progress? Do three things today to get off to a strong start.

Thing #1
Make a commitment. **What *one* change will you make in the next week?**

Write it down or add it to your task-tracking system —right now! This helps you build momentum for all the other changes.

Thing #2
Second, make a note in your calendar to **send me an update in six months**. The six-month mark is a chance for you to review your progress. I want to hear what's happened since you first read the book.

When the time comes, email me at
Karl@SakasAndCompany.com

I read every message and often share additional free resources.

Thing #3

Finally, think about your career history. Who was your best manager? Send them a quick thank-you email today.

It doesn't have to be fancy. Here's a cut-and-paste template:

> *Thanks for showing me how to be a good manager. Now that I lead a team myself, I finally appreciate the work you were doing back then to create a great experience for our team. I especially remember when you _____.*
> *Thank you for being a role model to me.*

Then send it. You'll make their day.

Don't have their contact info—or they've passed away? Take the time to write the note anyway. It'll help you clarify what you value as a leader, including areas where you want to improve.

Additional Resources

Ready to accelerate your progress? I've created a free set of tools, which you can download at **SakasAndCompany.com/teambook**

- Accountability template
- Layoff guide
- Performance Improvement Plan (PIP) template
- And new tools as I add them

Want additional resources? Here are some favorites:

- *Anything You Want* by Derek Sivers

- "Ask a Manager" blog by Alison Green at AskAManager.org

- Manager Tools website at Manager-Tools.com

- *Managing (Right) for the First Time* by David C. Baker

- *The HUMAN Brand* by Chris Malone and Susan T. Fiske

- *Turn the Ship Around!* by David L. Marquet

About the Author

Karl Sakas (@KarlSakas) helps agencies grow profitably, without the usual growing pains. Clients call him their "business therapist."

As president of global consulting firm Sakas & Company, Karl has advised agencies on six continents about operations, strategy, and leadership. He founded an online community with agencies in 50 countries.

Karl is the author of *The In-Demand Marketing Agency* and 200+ articles on agency management.

When he's not helping clients, Karl volunteers as a bartender on a 1930s railroad car, mixing martinis at 100 miles an hour. He lives in Raleigh, North Carolina.

Get free tips when you sign up for his email newsletter at <u>SakasAndCompany.com</u>

Want to contact Karl? Send an email to <u>Karl@SakasAndCompany.com</u>.

19471348R00038

Printed in Great Britain
by Amazon